Original title:
Beneath the Ocean's Breath

Copyright © 2025 Creative Arts Management OÜ
All rights reserved.

Author: Rafael Sterling
ISBN HARDBACK: 978-1-80587-453-9
ISBN PAPERBACK: 978-1-80587-923-7

The Pulse of the Abyss

Down where the fish wear tiny shoes,
Turtles dance with rhythmic snooze.
Octopus juggles with a grin,
While seaweed laughs, it's a win-win.

Crabs play checkers, what a sight,
Jellyfish float, oh what delight!
Starfish cheer, 'You can't lose!
Unless it's to that shark, who chews!'

Celestial Waves and Silent Depths

The waves roll in with a giddy laugh,
A dolphin's swim, a slippery path.
Seahorses twirl in sequined coats,
While whales crack jokes on tiny boats.

Coral reefs are nightclubs bright,
Where fish dance close and hold on tight.
"Hey, let's salsa!" the clownfish shout,
But the mermaids just roll their eyes and pout.

Mysteries of the Marine Veil

In kelp forests, creatures hold a chat,
"Did you hear that whoopee cushion spat?"
Giant squids with a flair for the jest,
Put sea cucumbers to the test!

Floating by, a crab in a hat,
Says, "I'm the captain, imagine that!"
But every time he takes the helm,
The ship starts spinning, oh what a realm!

Silhouette of the Submerged

At twilight's call, some fish regale,
Of lost adventures in a daring sail.
Pufferfish giggle, all puffed up,
"Who needs a drink? I'm fully sup!"

Nemo jokes with fins that twirl,
While angelfish dance, making pearls.
Crabs wear shades in the ocean's light,
Claiming they're stars of an undersea fight!

Dances of the Deep Blue

The jellyfish twirl in bright ballet,
They jig and they waltz, come join the fray!
With squishy moves, they float and glide,
In a sea of laughter, all take a ride.

The octopus shows off eight silly feet,
Doing the cha-cha to a coral beat!
A crab shuffles sideways, what a display,
Claws snap in rhythm, hip-hip-hooray!

Beneath the Tide's Embrace

A dolphin's flip makes everyone cheer,
Splashing water, spreading good cheer!
With a wink and a smile, it dives down low,
While sea turtles yell, "Hey, look at our show!"

A starfish plays poker, with clam shells laid,
While seahorses gossip in the seabed shade.
With bubbles as currency, they bet and laugh,
In this underwater world, they're having a blast!

Ocean's Heartbeat

The clownfish giggle, they wiggle with glee,
In anemone beds, they're full of esprit.
They pull silly faces, a funny parade,
Making their home a grand cabaret!

With a whale's deep chuckle, the bubbles arise,
Echoing laughter, a splashy surprise.
A song of the sea, in joyous refrain,
Where fish mingle freely, and fun is gained!

The Language of Seaweed

The seaweed whispers of secrets untold,
With sways and bends, both daring and bold.
It tickles the fish, they giggle and play,
In a dance of green waves, they twirl all day.

A porpoise joins in, with a twist and a spin,
Joining strange plants in a whirlpool grin.
They hold a grand party, with snacks from the tide,
In jokes made of bubbles, there's nothing to hide!

Lullabies of the Sea

Fish in pajamas, dancing with glee,
Octopus plays drums, a rockin' spree.
Starfish sing softly, a chorus so bright,
As whales hum lullabies through the night.

Seahorses twirl in a bubbly ballet,
Crabs do the cha-cha, come join the fray.
Jellyfish float by, all wiggly and sweet,
With clams clapping shells to the funky beat.

Shadows in the Brine

A squid with a hat, what a comical sight,
He juggles the shells, oh what pure delight!
Eels in a line, they're telling a joke,
But the punchline's lost in a bubble of smoke.

A turtle in shades rolls by with a grin,
Chasing a plankton that thinks it can win.
With laughter so loud, the seaweed does sway,
As fish share a tale of the one that got away.

Coral Dreams and Rippling Secrets

Clams huddle close for a gossiping spree,
While dolphins play tag with the driftwood tree.
Coral gardens flourish, so colorful and bright,
As crabs wear sunglasses, feeling just right.

Anemone dances with a starry-eyed smile,
As shrimp throw a party, it's now quite the style.
With laughter and joy, they all sing a tune,
And dance with the bubbles, beneath the bright moon.

Underwater Reveries

A fish with a bow tie swims past in a rush,
While seaweed giggles, oh what a hush!
Hippos in flippers, they waddle around,
With turtles on scooters, making quite a sound.

The playful sea otters hold hands in a ring,
While all of the mussels just sit there and cling.
Together they share in this wacky parade,
Remembering that laughter will never quite fade.

Hidden in the Hollows of Waves

Seahorses gossip with dreamy stares,
While jellyfish jive in polka-dot flares.
Barnacles grumble like old grumpy men,
While starfish hold court with a glittering pen.

The octopus winks, a sly little tease,
As crabs pull pranks on the soft, sandy breeze.
With each silly swell, a laugh rides the foam,
In the watery world, everyone's home.

Tendrils of History in Saltwater

Fish in tuxedos, they prance and they sashay,
Whales wear bow ties, it's quite the display.
A clam has a secret, tucked under its shell,
While dolphins exchange jokes—oh, do tell!

Pirates past snooze beneath kelp's bright embrace,
While sea cucumbers laze in their place.
Gorging on stories, the waves softly roar,
With history teasing from the ocean's floor.

Foundations of the Dark-Hued Depths

Where shadows dance like the flick of a tail,
Anemones giggle, they never will pale.
The grouchy old grouper thinks he's the king,
But even he chuckles at the jokes that they sing.

Eels with their quirks, twist and twirl in delight,
While sea turtles argue who's fastest in flight.
Caves full of laughter, echoing through,
As guppies exchanged knows a thing or two.

Where Currents Sing and Dance

The bubbles are bursting with untold jokes,
As sea urchins chatter like mischievous folks.
Puffers in bowler hats puff out their cheeks,
While the wily old octopus plays hide-and-seek.

Turtles in tutus glide here and there,
While seaweed sways like it hasn't a care.
Harmony hoots from the depth's grassy glen,
In this underwater ball, it's fun once again!

Reflections in the Blue Veil

In the deep, where fish do twirl,
A crab lost his bright white pearl.
He danced and sang, oh what a sight,
A fashion faux pas in the moonlight.

Seahorses giggle, a bubble bath,
While clams file lawsuits for their wrath.
Octopus juggles, what a show,
With eight arms waving, 'Look at me go!'

Secrets of the Salty Expanse

A dolphin lost its sense of humor,
Swapping jokes with a grouchy bloomer.
The pufferfish puffed, trying to show,
That a dad joke's the best way to blow.

Starfish tell tales of a caper grand,
When they stole a net, oh isn't that planned?
The turtles roll their eyes in the light,
Saying 'We've heard this one every night!'

The Lure of the Sunken Treasures

A chest of gold in a ship's old knee,
Draws in fish with a shiny decree.
But upon a closer fishy glance,
It's just a can from a sailor's dance!

The mermaids laugh as they comb their hair,
While a wise old whale gives a little stare.
'Not everything shiny has gold inside!'
He rolls his eyes, then goes for a ride.

Songs of the Silent Schools

In the coral halls where silence sings,
Fish gossip and spread their little flings.
A school of tuna with gossip to share,
They giggle and wiggle without a care.

Squids play charades with elaborate flair,
While plankton disguise in a stack of hair.
The seaweed sways to their silly rhymes,
Creating a scene for hilarious times.

The Forgotten Echo of Shells

Once a clam danced, oh what a sight,
With a crab that grinned, in the pale moonlight.
They twirled and swirled, both so very proud,
Until a wave knocked them straight from their crowd.

A fish swam by, giggling with glee,
Said, "You're not alone; join the conch and me!"
Together they laughed, creating a scene,
Of shells making music, quite the marine routine.

Dreams Cradled in Kelp

In the sway of the sea, the seaweed dreams,
A starfish wished for legs and candy streams.
The bubbles laughed, all jiggly and round,
While seahorses pranced, spinning 'round and 'round.

Kelp beds whispered secrets, not fit for ears,
As fish told tales that tickled their peers.
With giggles and splashes, they spun a big web,
Of silly sea tales, like a watery celeb.

Floating on the Breath of the Current

A jolly old dolphin, with a toothy grin,
Swam circles around a very chill fin.
"Come join the parade, it's a seaweed fest!"
But the grouchy old turtle just needed his rest.

Octopus offered a dance with new flair,
While the clownfish joked, "I once lost my hair!"
They laughed and bubbled, joyously loud,
Floating through currents, a merry sea crowd.

Lanterns in the Dark Water

In the deep where the light rarely tricks,
Glowworms had parties, with fancy sea flicks.
An anglerfish joked, "You light up my life!"
While a flute-playing shrimp snuck off with a knife.

They twinkled and shimmied, a glowing delight,
Creating a dance that sparked in the night.
With laughter like bubbles, their spirits so free,
Lanterns of light formed a zany sea spree.

Time's Embrace in Aquatic Graces

A jellyfish twirls, looking so grand,
But trip on a wave, it's hard to stand.
Sea turtles snicker as they glide by,
"Watch your step, mate! Oh my, oh my!"

Fish in their school, they gossip and tease,
"Did you see Gary? He forgot to sneeze!"
Crabs have a dance, a sideways parade,
While seahorses chuckle at the moves they've made.

Corals bright hues like a painter's spree,
But watch for the octopus – he's quite the spree!
"What's your splash, friend? Got a gig to share?"
He winks with a shrug, a jet of cool air.

Starfish debate the best sunning spots,
While clams stay tucked, avoiding their thoughts.
Nature's a show, the sea's never dull,
With slapstick ballet from every sea moll.

The Ocean's Palette of Enchantment

Colors collide under the sun's glow,
A clownfish prances, putting on a show.
"Dude, check my stripes! Aren't they a hit?"
While shrimp in the back says, "You're full of it!"

Anemones wave in the currents so bright,
"What's up, my friends? Ready for a bite?"
But seagulls swoop down with a laugh and a caw,
"We'll grab your lunch; look at us in awe!"

Bubbles burst forth like giggles galore,
As dolphins flip high and land on the shore.
"We're just a splash seal! Come join the fun!"
"Always a party; we're never done!"

Urchins discuss, oh the latest sea trends,
"Did you see last week? The foam had great bends!"
With starry-eyed dreams of the tides' magical sway,
They ponder the colors of waters' ballet.

Whispers of History in Seafoam

Old tales are told in the briny deep,
Where fishy folks gather, secrets to keep.
"Did you hear about the anchor who danced?"
"Oh, give it a rest! It had no chance!"

Barnacles chuckle, their home on a ship,
"We're royalty here, just look at our grip!"
While dolphins converse of the legends they know,
"Fables of ancient, let's put on a show!"

Coral reefs murmur with gossip and glee,
"What's new in the rocks? Did you see to the sea?"
But crabs tell a story of a treasure chest lost,
"It's just full of shells, and maybe some frost!"

With a flick of the tail and a splash in the spray,
The creatures continue their lyrical play.
In the salty sea tales, laughter abounds,
As history whispers with shimmering sounds.

Shadows of the Tide

Jellyfish dance with a wink,
Caught in a seaweed's clink.
Crabs in tuxedos strut and preen,
Laughing at fish who can't keep clean.

Octopuses play hide and seek,
In coral castles, quite unique.
Starfish giggle, make a bed,
While seahorses wear hats on their head.

Seashells gossip on the shore,
Whispering tales of ocean's lore.
Fish with funny faces lurk,
Behind every rock, they do their work.

The tide rolls in with a playful push,
Gathering up sea foam in a rush.
With each wave, a new surprise,
Under water, those silly guys!

Unraveled by the Current

A fish with glasses reads a book,
Says to a crab, "Come take a look!"
But the crab's busy, lost in a snack,
Pasta made from a tiny clam's pack.

A dolphin jokes, "What's your best line?"
A flatfish replies, "I can't define!"
They chuckle and swim with a spin,
Splashing around with a toothy grin.

Turtles race with a slow-motion flair,
While a starfish tries to style its hair.
Giggles echo through the sea foam,
As each creature finds its own home.

Oh what fun in the bright blue deep,
Where laughter bubbles and secrets keep.
With every wave comes a funny tale,
Riding the current, we set sail!

Pelagic Dreams and Whirling Currents

In a whirlpool of dreams, fish take flight,
Turtles stretch out, feeling quite right.
A narwhal sings off-key in glee,
Forgetting the words to the ocean's spree.

Clownfish paint with colors bright,
Creating rainbows in the light.
Anglerfish with a glowing lure,
Says, "Why not? Let's not be sure!"

Bubbles rise with giggles and cheek,
As whales form a band that's unique.
Seashells snap their tiny claps,
In the wacky waves of underwater naps.

With currents swirling, chaos ensues,
Sea cucumbers form a dance in shoes.
A medley of laughter, a splash of fun,
In these watery dreams, we never run!

The Sea's Melancholy

The seaweed sways with a sullen sigh,
As fishes giggle and pass by.
A lonely clam wears a frown,
Wishing for a friend to come around.

A shark tried a joke, but no one laughed,
Just floating jelly, their mood quite daft.
"Why so glum?" a dolphin inquired,
"It's tough to be cool when moods are tired."

Crabs in a line march to the beat,
While sea otters whirl in a whimsical feat.
They balance rocks with all their might,
Bringing cheer to the fading light.

Yet a starfish whispered in secret retreat,
"Sometimes silly can't be beat."
So they rallied and danced in a merry row,
Turning the blues to a wonderful show!

In the Grip of the Ocean's Embrace

A jellyfish wobbled by, oh my!
With arms like noodles, it waved hi.
The fish all giggled in a school,
As bubbles popped; that was the rule.

A crab in sunglasses snapped a grin,
Wiggling its claws, ready to spin.
The octopus tried to dance a jig,
But tangled up in seaweed big.

A whale waved gently, what a creature!
Making the dolphins roar with laughter.
They splashed around, a playful scene,
In this soggy underwater routine.

The sea turtles raced, all in a line,
But got distracted by a plankton dine.
They rolled and tumbled, what a race!
In this comical, wet, wild place.

The Dance of Flickering Fins

Twinkling fish in a crazy dance,
Swirling and twirling, oh what a chance!
A sardine slipped on a slick sea floor,
And surprisingly knocked on a clam's door.

Seahorses strutted in snappy suits,
Like dapper gents off to chase some hoots.
But tripped on bubbles, came tumbling down,
Oh, the laughable chaos, the lost fish crown!

Flounders flipped in a silly beat,
While starfish cheered from their cozy seat.
They clapped their arms, what a delight,
As eels joined in, swirling left and right.

A conch shell giggled with a big round face,
As everyone danced in bubbly grace.
In this underwater gala, full of cheer,
Everyone's welcome; join, never fear!

The Unseen Choir Beneath

A concert of bubbles floated by,
The mermaids giggled, oh me, oh my!
With fins and shells, they made a sound,
A bubble-burst symphony all around.

Clams hummed low, while scallops sang,
Their bouncy beats made the seaweed hang.
But the sea cucumber led off-key,
Causing nearby fish to swim with glee.

A starfish played the conch with flair,
But forgot the lyrics, causing despair.
The octopus joined, added some beat,
Dancing in rhythm on wobbly feet.

As the last note drifted to the blue,
A crab bowed down; what a show it flew!
With laughter echoing through the sea,
An unseen choir, wild and free.

Insights from the Ancient Reefs

In coral castles, wisdom sways,
Fish philosophers share their days.
An old turtle spoke of times so grand,
Of bubbles, giggles, and fine sea sand.

Clownfish jester told a funny tale,
Of a sea slug that learned to sail.
With tiny fins and a great big sigh,
He fluttered off, kissing the sky.

A shrimp gave advice on how to dance,
With a little shake and a silly prance.
All gathered round for tips and tricks,
To loosen up and share their kicks.

As waves carried stories far and wide,
These ancient reefs became the guide.
With humor and laughter, they found their groove,
In this colorful world, they continued to move.

Echoes in the Aqua Canopy

Fish in tuxedos dance with flair,
Jellybeans float without a care.
Octopuses juggle, oh what a sight,
Crabs in top hats go out at night.

Seahorses giggle, swapping tall tales,
While clowns in seaweed wear their gales.
Nemo's lost again, where could he be?
Oh wait, he's stuck in a crabby marquee!

Starfish learn to foxtrot with ease,
And sea cucumbers bounce like peas.
The dolphins are laughing, comically bright,
As they blow bubbles, pure delight!

Mermaids are grinning, for they won the race,
With mermen tripping all over the place.
As laughter erupts in the watery show,
All join the fun in the blue below.

Shadows of the Coral Kingdom

In the realm where the corals reside,
Clownfish are jesters, take it in stride.
With patches of colors, they strut with a grin,
Each day's a party, let laughter begin!

Turtles in shades take a sunbathing break,
Sea slugs with sass, giving others a shake.
Anemone's beauty attracts all the fuss,
While eels in bow ties make quite the fuss.

Sardines form conga lines by the reef,
While crabs kick back, enjoying their beef.
"Can you catch me?" the pufferfish teases,
But trips on seaweed, oh how it sneezes!

It's a rollercoaster in the coral parade,
With fish in formation, a splashy charade.
The sea floor is bouncing with laughter and cheer,
As shadows play games, year after year.

Lullabies of the Ocean Floor

Sleepy sea stars hum a soft tune,
While snails on a stroll dance under the moon.
The seaweed sways, a gentle caress,
While octopuses wear their pajamas to bless.

Anglerfish flash with a grin so bright,
Scaring poor shrimp out of sheer fright.
Walruses snore, deeply they dream,
As bubbles rise up to join in the scheme.

The seashells gossip, sharing their lore,
While hermit crabs sneak through the door.
Each lap of the tide is a rhythm so sweet,
While clams tap their feet to the sand's heartbeat.

And in this calm, the funny creeps in,
As dolphins play doctor with a big, goofy grin.
The night holds laughter, tucked in each wave,
As the ocean's lullaby keeps the fun brave.

Rhythms of the Subaqueous World

Bubbles are rising with silly sounds,
Where fish are jiving without bounds.
The grouper sings out with a wobbly tune,
While seagulls dance under the sun and moon.

Clams keep secrets, oh such a fuss,
And sea turtles chuckle while riding the bus.
"Wait, hold on!" cries a fish with glee,
As they tumble and roll, wild and free.

A race with the current, they splash all around,
In this merry world where joy can be found.
Mermaids in crowns throw confetti of shells,
While giggles and bubbles ring like sweet bells.

The beat of the waves is a cue to all play,
As fish play tag, what a glorious day!
A tangle of laughter, a twist of a fin,
In the undersea world, let the fun begin!

The Driftwood Chronicles

Floating logs tell tales of fluff,
Of fish who bicker and dance in stuff.
A crab once wore a tiny hat,
In hopes to charm a nearby brat.

Was it a wave or just a prank?
As seaweed tickles, fish all drank.
A clam does karaoke each night,
While starfish cheer in pure delight.

A seagull tried to start a club,
With barnacles as a cool hub.
But all they did was fallout snack,
And gossip behind the captain's back.

In each driftwood log, laughter's key,
With barnacle jokes, so carefree.
So join the crew, and take a sit,
At the ocean's shore, it's quite a hit!

Secrets Quietly Archived by the Sea

The sand knows secrets, whispers so loud,
Of jellyfish pranks that made a crowd.
A dolphin laughed when a seal slipped,
And the whole town together quipped.

Coral reefs hold tales of woe,
As clowns, the fish, steal the show.
A mermaid threw a fishy ball,
But missed her catch, oh what a fall!

Clams gossip wildly, spread the word,
About the octopus who danced absurd.
With eight-armed boogie and flair so grand,
He won the title of sea's best band.

So dive where giggles stir the tide,
For hidden jokes the waves can't hide.
Just listen close to what they share,
In salty breezes, laughter's rare!

An Odyssey Within Aquatic Shadows

Fish in tuxedos find their mates,
While turtles obsess over dinner dates.
A wave who burped made all fish flee,
Creating ripples in comedy.

The sea's a stage where laughter blooms,
With crabs in costumes playing tunes.
A whale once thought he'd tell a joke,
But the punchline sank like a heavy cloak.

Tangled in seaweed, an eel gets stuck,
Yelling, "Help! I'm just out of luck!"
A shrimp advised with a wise little grin,
"Just wiggle and jiggle, you'll surely win!"

Giant clams clap to the rhythm tight,
While plankton dances till the night.
So swim along, join in the cheer,
For laughter echoes throughout the year!

Tales from the Veil of Water

Bubbles burst with a sound so funny,
As mermaids practice their acts for money.
A sea urchin tried to tell a story,
But ended up in a glittering gory.

Octopuses hold their arms up high,
To juggle fishes who swim by.
A crab in flip-flops danced on rocks,
Joking, "Who needs these old crocs?"

Anemones giggle at the shrimp's wild luck,
As they squabble over who runs the muck.
With slippery laughs, the sea critters play,
Bringing joy in a bubbly ballet.

So come enjoy this underwater charade,
Where fishy jokes never seem to fade.
In every wave, laughter swells and flows,
Through salty air, the merry rhythm grows!

Voyage into the Blue Abyss

A jellyfish danced, a silly sight,
With tentacles swaying, left and right.
The fish all laughed, in scales so bright,
While pirates played cards, what a delight!

A crab in a hat thought he was grand,
Telling tall tales of treasure planned.
But when he stood up, fell in the sand,
With a gentle ripple, his dreams were canned!

The octopus waved with too many hands,
Juggling the seaweed, making grand stands.
He slipped on a fish, failed his fine plans,
And splashed all the clams with slippery strands!

So if you set sail on this giggling spree,
Expect some mischief from the creatures you see.
With laughter and whimsy, just follow the glee,
In a world where fun swims wild and free!

Depths of the Unseen

Down in the deep, where the shadows play,
A squid in a tuxedo had a ball today.
He twirled and he whirled, what a strange display,
Who knew that sea life could dance this way?

A whale with a top hat sang a tune,
Its voice echoed back, oh, what a boon!
But a dolphin jumped in with a splash too soon,
Sending the jellyfish flying like balloons!

A grouchy old eel looked on with disdain,
"Why all this fuss? It's driving me insane!"
But every fish laughed, again and again,
His frown disappeared—he couldn't complain!

So down in the darkness, where laughter ignites,
The quirks of the ocean bring joy to the sights.
Just join in the fun, let go of your plights,
And dance with the critters, by day and by night!

Whispers of the Tidal Deep

Where the coral blooms and the bubbles rise,
A starfish complained about fishy lies.
"I swear I once saw a whale in disguise,
Wearing a mustache, oh, how time flies!"

An anemone giggled, swaying so spry,
Telling the tale of the shy little guy.
"A crab with a mic, under moonlit sky,
Rapped about sandcastles—oh, my oh my!"

The seaweed swayed, trying to join in,
But tangled its roots and fell with a spin.
"Just swim with the rhythm, let's all be kin,
We'll laugh at our blunders, come on, let's begin!"

So listen to whispers, dance 'round the reef,
Where the clams are comedians, bring joy, not grief.
In the deep, lively world, all troubles are brief,
Play along with the ocean, where laughter's belief!

Secrets of the Submerged Realm

In a realm of bubbles, the fish raised a cheer,
A seahorse dressed up as a knight with no fear.
He charged at a bubble—oh dear, oh dear!
But he bounced right back, laughing without a tear!

A clownfish, the jester, threw seaweed confetti,
"Join in the fun, grab a friend, don't be petty!"
But a hermit crab frowned, feeling all ready,
To march in his shell like a crustacean yeti!

An octopus chef served calamari flies,
But they all turned out to be some funky pies.
With laughter erupting, they entered surprise,
Who knew gooey snacks could be such a prize?

So wander these waters, embrace all their quirks,
In this bubbling laughter, away with the jerks.
Where fish wear sombreros and play silly perks,
Find joy in the deep, with its giggles and smirks!

Whispers of the Tide

The fish all gather, gossip with glee,
"Did you hear that? A crab stole my sea!"
A dolphin chuckles, flips in delight,
"That crab's got moves, he danced all night!"

A starfish sighed, "I just want to chill,"
While turtles argue, "Who's got the skill?"
The seaweed sways with the biggest grin,
As waves roll in, the laughter begins!

An octopus juggles, just for a laugh,
While clams take bets on the mermaid's bath.
Fish turn to sharks, saying, "Don't be mean!"
In this ocean world, they're all part of the scene!

From reefs to the depths, it's a comedy show,
Where jellyfish dance with a jellyfish glow.
Each bubble that rises, a giggle it brings,
In currents of fun, it's the ocean that sings!

Secrets in the Deep

There's a whale who sings, out of tune so loud,
Even sea turtles flee, calling for the crowd.
"Please stop!" they plead, but he just can't hear,
His bass voice echoes, spreading the cheer!

A crab once claimed, he could dance like a pro,
But his moves were more like a soft sinking show.
Anemones giggled, "Do we smell stinky?"
As fish held their noses, feeling quite dinky!

A sunken ship boasts of treasure and gold,
But all that's inside is just a big mold.
The treasures are jokes, and the crew's all a hoot,
With sea monsters roaring, they're always astute!

In the darkness lurk secrets, both silly and wild,
Where octopuses prank every unsuspecting child.
With laughter and bubbles, the deep holds a dream,
Of wacky fish tales and a glowing, bright seam!

Echoes of Lost Mariners

There once was a sailor, quite lost in his quest,
He followed a seagull, who told him to rest.
He found a lone buoy, thinking it clear,
But it creaked and groaned, offering no cheer!

A clam let out puns, a real comic chap,
The sailors groaned loudly, "Come on, take a nap!"
Their maps full of fish, all swimming away,
With laughter they wandered, lost in the sway.

With echoes of footsteps on decks made of sand,
They twirled with the dolphins, quite gallantly planned.
The compass spun 'round, and the wind gave a tease,
Tickling their senses with oceanic breeze!

The ghost of a captain, still searching for crew,
Found a whale who danced, and said, "Me and you!"
Together they sailed, in this nautical jest,
Lost but not lonely, just part of the quest!

Currents of the Forgotten

In currents so swift, where the sea turtles glide,
A lost pirate's hat took quite the wild ride.
With fishy companions who loved to parade,
They turned it to fashion, a trendy charade!

A jellyfish wore it, like a crown on her head,
While crabs took selfies, all fears put to bed.
Sea urchins rolled laughter, in bubbles they soared,
With echoes of joy, they were never ignored!

The currents all bubble with secrets untold,
As creatures concoct tales from the brave to the bold.
A whirlpool of laughter, a splash of delight,
In this whimsical water, everything's bright!

So when you dive deep, look for these fun,
In a world where the currents tickle and run.
With a wink and a nudge, they'll invite you to play,
A splash of good humor, forever to stay!

The Call of the Undercurrent

A fish tried to dance, oh what a sight,
He tripped on a shell and gave quite a fright.
Octopus chuckled, "Don't be so rash!"
While seahorses giggled, caught in a splash.

A crab joined the party, with a shake of his claws,
He boogied all night, breaking all the laws.
The jellyfish floated, with a wobble so grand,
Saying, "Let's groove, it's a jellyfish band!"

The tuna brought snacks, a feast like no other,
While starfish enjoyed it, then danced with each other.
The turtle rolled in, with a grin ear to ear,
"Why did the fish cross? Just to get here!"

Laughter echoed deep, from reef to the tide,
As the ocean's weirdos laughed and just sighed.
They spun and they swirled, with joy all around,
In this silly-blue kingdom, where giggles abound!

Under Currents of Timelessness

A dolphin once wore a bright party hat,
He said, "I'm the champ, all you fish, now chat!"
But a clownfish quipped, with a wink and a grin,
"Bubbles don't count, but let's all dive in!"

An octopus popped up with eight arms to share,
"Who needs a dance partner when I've got flair?"
The seaweed swayed like it knew all the moves,
While crabs in the corner perfected their grooves.

A narwhal showed up with a sparkly horn,
And shouted, "Let's party! I'll play till the morn!"
But a turtle just shrugged, "I'm a bit more slow,
I'll twerk with the current, but let's take it slow!"

Then came all the fish, with a whimsy-filled cheer,
As the ocean erupted, with laughter not fear.
"Let's wiggle and giggle, from end to end!"
In these waters of joy, every wave is a friend!

A Mosaic of Blue Silence

In bubbles of laughter, a shrimp made a throne,
"I rule this deep realm, though I'm just made of foam!"
A seahorse replied, with a flip of her tail,
"Your rule is quite silly, let's set off and sail!"

From coral to kelp, the party took flight,
With angelfish dancing till late in the night.
A walrus came wobbly, with a pie on a plate,
"Who's hungry for cake? You all should create!"

The swordfish popped in, with a wink and a flash,
"Who ordered a swim with a side of some trash?"
With laughter rippling, and glee taking hold,
In this underwater realm, stories unfold.

So raise up your fins, feel the giggles arise,
In currents of joy, wear your fun disguise.
For deep in the blue, magic spins all around,
In this comical realm, happiness is found!

Under the Gaze of Ocean Stars

A crab with a moustache, oh what a delight,
Made the fish laugh till the morning light.
A shrimp threw confetti with a wink of her eye,
While jellyfish turned, with a luminous sigh.

A weathered old turtle recalled tales of old,
"Back in my day, we were brave and bold!"
But a pufferfish piped in, with a pop and a jig,
"Now it's about fun, we're all just too big!"

The skates pulled a prank, with a splash and a flop,
Turning some fish into gigglers nonstop.
They danced in a circle, round bubbles and blues,
In the magic of waters, they danced without shoes.

So here in this haven, where laughter is gold,
The secrets of sea are both silly and bold.
With each wave that rolls in, let your worries escape,
For beneath all the laughter, wonderful shapes!

The Gentle Pulse of the Sea

The waves dance and prance, oh what a sight,
A fish in a tuxedo, ready for the night.
Seahorses playing tag, giggling with glee,
Who knew the ocean had such a spree?

The jellyfish disco, glowing so bright,
They twirl and they twist, what a marvelous night!
A crab with a top hat, a starfish in gold,
Their stories of ocean, hilariously told.

Octopuses juggling, a true circus show,
While clams sing their ballads, all buried below.
The ocean's a party, with laughter so grand,
From the depths of the sea to the warm, sunlit sand.

So join in the fun, don your flippers and dive,
In this world of mirth, the sea comes alive.
With bubbles and giggles, let's float and we'll sway,
For the ocean's heartbeat is here to play!

Fantasies from the Ocean's Heart

In the depths of water, where mermaids do dwell,
They swap silly stories, and giggle quite well.
With fish riding bicycles, just take a glance,
The coral reefs bursting with whimsical dance.

A dolphin with mischief, jumps high in the air,
While a clam tells a joke, nobody's there.
With seaweed confetti floating all around,
Who knew the ocean held laughter so profound?

The whales make a symphony, off-key and absurd,
Singing tunes about turtles, flying like birds.
All the creatures chuckle, it's joy-filled and bright,
In this underwater realm, where everything's light.

With bubbles of laughter, they bubble and burst,
Reminding us all to embrace our own thirst.
For fun under waves is just a splash away,
In the fantasy sea, where we laugh and we play!

Beneath the Tide's Embrace

Tangled in kelp, a fish makes a face,
Wiggling with laughter, a comedic chase.
The starfish gets startled, oh what a fright,
When it tickles a turtle, laughing in delight.

An octopus quips, 'I've got eight arms to spare!'
While sea anemones joke, 'We do it with flair!'
A crab in a tutu, what a quirky sight,
In the ocean's embrace, everything feels light.

Manta rays glide with a twist and a turn,
As the sea cucumbers wait for their turn.
With giggles and bubbles, the currents do sway,
In this whimsical world, we'll laugh and we play.

So dance with the currents and let worries flee,
For life under waves is the best kind of spree.
With the tide as our friend, there's joy all around,
In the ocean's embrace, laughter knows no bound!

Anemone's Gentle Caress

In a garden of sea, where the colors collide,
Anemones play peek-a-boo, filled with pride.
A clownfish complains, 'This tickles too much!'
With giggles galore, the sea's soft to touch.

The sea turtles race, can they go the distance?
But they stop for a snack, forgetting existence.
With a splash and a pop, oh what a scene,
The ocean's a big bowl of jellybean!

As dolphins do flips, in the shimmering spray,
The ocean's a stage for the absurd play.
An audience of fish, in colors so bold,
The jokes they have written are legends retold.

So let's spread our fins, with humor we'll sail,
In the vast salty blue, where laughter prevails.
With currents of joy, and waves that enchant,
The sea's gentle caress is a giggly dance!

Aquatic Whispers Through Seaweed

In seaweed forests, fish do dance,
They wiggle their tails, give shells a chance.
A crab in a tux, with style so grand,
Recites a poem, clapping his hand.

With bubbles that giggle, they softly speak,
The octopus jokes, his ink leaves a streak.
A turtle plays hide and seeks with a ray,
While seahorses strut, showing off all day.

Waves are the laughter, the tides are the glee,
As dolphins do flips, oh what a sight to see!
Starfish are stargazers, resting with flair,
While mantas wear capes, like they just don't care.

In this underwater rave, the fun won't cease,
For every fish furthers the joy and peace.
So join in the frolic, let loose and unwind,
In the world under waves, hilarity you'll find.

Where Moonlight Touches the Seafloor

Moonbeams cascade like a silver stream,
Fish in tuxedos swim, ready to gleam.
Anemones giggle as they twirl with a whirl,
While crabs on the dance floor just wiggle and twirl.

The shrimp wear their best, with colors so bright,
They cha-cha through currents, a comical sight.
Oysters gossip, their pearls held so tight,
While squids juggle shells under soft starlight.

Bubbles rise up, like laughter in flight,
The parrotfish chortles, what a delight!
Even the barnacles join in the spree,
As nighttime unfolds, it's a real jubilee!

So sway with the rhythm of the tide's gentle kiss,
In waters where shadows often turn to bliss.
Frolic under the moon, let worries unmoor,
And dance to the laughter from deep to the shore.

Echoes of the Forgotten Tide

In the depths where echoes swim and play,
A clam tells a joke that's far too cliché.
While fish roll their eyes, they twist and they spin,
As sea cucumbers laugh, amazed at their grin.

"Why did the jellyfish cross the sea?"
To show an old dolphin, "It's all about glee!"
Shells crack a smile, tiny snails cheer them on,
As waves tell their secrets 'til break of the dawn.

The flounder wears glasses, reading a book,
He chuckles aloud at the sights that he took.
Old sharks share their tales, both silly and bold,
While a clownfish snickers, "Come on, it's old!"

In currents of laughter, the sea starts to sing,
With giggles and bubbles of joy that they bring.
So treasure the tides that once danced so free,
For laughter transcends, as deep as you see.

The Luminous Path of Coral

Corals glow brightly, a vivid parade,
With a clownfish's antics, all fears start to fade.
The sea urchins chuckle, their spines in a twist,
As clownfish claim crowns, "We simply insist!"

Eels in their jackets, they shimmy and slide,
As anemones giggle, lost in the tide.
"Why don't we fight?" says a grouchy old turbot,
"I'd much rather dance, let's have a big showboat!"

Shrimps wear their hats, all decked out for flair,
They spin in a whirl, though no one would care.
A pufferfish blushes when he starts to puff,
"Oh, darling, it's hard to look cute when you're tough!"

So gather your laughter, your smiles, and jest,
In the underwater realm, humor's the best.
Where colors unite in a dance full of cheer,
In the luminous coral, our joy is quite clear.

Silent Serenade of the Sea

A fish in a tux, with a bow and a grin,
Sipping on seaweed, where do we begin?
He hums to the tides, with a giggle, a splash,
Dancing with crabs, in a turtle's mustache.

The jellyfish twirls in a wobbly flight,
Wearing bright colors, a party tonight!
With shimm'ring scales, they all start to twine,
Cracking up whales, who just can't align.

Seahorses spin like they're stuck in a trance,
Making a splash in their wobbly dance.
They share silly jokes with a wink and a wave,
As bubbles of laughter escape from the cave.

An octopus juggles with shells and some glee,
While sharks roll their eyes at the ruckus, oh me!
In this wacky world where the sea creatures meet,
The laughter and fun make the ocean complete.

A Symphony of Aquatic Whispers

In a coral castle, the clownfish invite,
To a concert of bubbles that pop with delight.
The sea anemone joins with a bop,
While hermit crabs shuffle, they'll never stop!

The conch shells echo with sounds oh so silly,
As starfish dance lightly, looking quite frilly.
With sea cucumbers grinning just so,
They rattle their bodies, putting on a show.

Dolphins are diving, all sparkling and bright,
Playing tag with the sunbeams, oh what a sight!
They serenade fish with a flip and a twist,
In the water ballet, nobody's missed.

As the seaweed sways beneath this grand bruhaha,
Every creature sings with a playful caw-caw.
With laughter like bubbles, the music will soar,
In the ocean's embrace, we just can't ask for more!

Secrets of the Surging Depths

Down in the deep, where the laughter just glows,
A whale shares secrets of love and of woes.
With a flip of a tail, he tells of romance,
As toaster fish giggle and join in the dance.

The eels slither past with a wiggle and tease,
While anglerfish snickers, if you catch their freeze.
They flash little lights, making night feel like day,
As squids throw confetti, in their own kooky way.

Manta rays glide in their elegant arcs,
Composing their sonnets beneath sea grass parks.
While turtles are laughing with glee, very loud,
Their shells like a drum, creating a crowd.

Whats the gossip, so juicy and bright?
A clownfish debates with a shrimp, what a sight!
In the depths of the blue, it's a raucous retreat,
Where everyone's welcome to dance on the beat!

The Underwater Poets

Gathered in silence, the poets convene,
With ink made of plankton, they're ready to glean.
The otters bring shells, as their paper and pen,
While seahorses scribble again and again.

They giggle and chuckle, crafting lines with a twist,
Mixing up rhymes that nobody missed.
The crabs get it rolling with pinch and with prance,
While dolphins dip low, throwing in their romance.

Mollusks recite with their mouths full of snacks,
While fish nibble on words like a poet's hard facts.
With laughter so loud, it shakes sand from the reef,
These underwater bards spread joy beyond belief.

As bubbles rise up, like ideas set free,
The sea holds their secrets, just wild as can be.
Casting nets made of laughter, in verses, they blend,
In this ocean of whimsy, where fun has no end.

Clarity in the Depth of Shadows

A crab in a tux, doing a jig,
Flippers about, it's quite the gig.
A fish with a tie, oh what a sight,
Dancing down here in the pale moonlight.

The jellyfish floats, all sparkly and round,
Swaying and swishing like it's party-bound.
A seaweed wig points, 'Look at me, folks!'
While nearby the octopus giggles and chokes.

A dolphin with shades rides the tide with flair,
Slick as a whistle without a care.
The anglerfish grins with its glowing lure,
"Who wants to join my dinner tour?"

With the laughter of bubbles, the joys are immense,
In this underwater world of pure nonsense.
So come join the fun, grab your gear,
And swim with the quirks that make us cheer!

The Siren's Call from the Marianas

A mermaid sings with a voice like silk,
Offering treasures, and cups of milk.
Fish stop to listen, their scales all a-shine,
While sea turtles munch on the kelp divine.

But what's that smell? Is it seaweed stew?
Or just a whale that misplaced its shoe?
The siren winks with a playful grin,
'Come closer, my friends, let the fun begin!'

The octopus juggles shells by the bay,
Squeezing in humor between each ballet.
With sea cucumbers stacked in a tower,
The crowd is in stitches, we laugh for an hour.

So heed the call if you want a surprise,
Just watch your step, mind your eyes!
For the sea is a jokester, both wise and bright,
With winks and with giggles, it's pure delight!

Tempest and Tranquility Below

The waves come crashing in funny ways,
With fishes who wear protective gaze.
A seahorse sneezes, it snorts like a pro,
While starfish giggle, all aglow.

There's a clam in a cape, feeling like hot stuff,
Trying to impress with its shiny rough.
"I'm the hero!" it shouts, while the others laugh loud,
As the crab rolls its eyes at this flamboyant crowd.

With jellybeans floating like clouds down here,
The sea cucumber dances without a care.
The puffer fish balloons with a pop and a fizz,
"Oh, is that my lunch? Oh, yes, that is!"

Though tempests rumble and currents may clash,
The wild underwater antics create quite a flash.
So let's hold our breath and dive into the show,
Where laughter is ample, and joyfreely flows!

Secrets Held by the Sea Sponges

Beneath the waves with secrets galore,
The sponges conspire, oh what a score!
They whisper and giggle, their tales quite absurd,
Of a fish who once flew, it's simply unheard!

"Did you hear the news?" one sponge starts to say,
"The clownfish debuted its own cabaret!"
With tubes all a-twitch, they gather 'round tight,
To hear every detail about that wild night.

The anemones turn, with colors so bright,
As squids throw confetti, what a wonderful sight!
Each tale gets taller, sparking such glee,
"What's next?" asks the sponge, "A talkative sea?"

So come share a laugh with these spongy folks,
Where tales are as wild as the best of jokes.
For in the depths, with silliness blessed,
There's magic and laughter, and joy at its best!

Ballad of the Silent Waters

A fish with a hat took a dive,
He claimed he was born to survive.
But juggling seaweed was tough,
Oh, this fish thinks he's so buff!

The crabs threw a party, quite loud,
With shells used as cups, oh so proud.
But one crab danced out of line,
He stumbled, said, 'I'm just fine!'

A starfish wearing socks made a scene,
He twirled in the sea like a queen.
His shiny shell got all the cheers,
But folks, quite honest, had some fears.

With laughter that bubbles and sways,
The sea critters play in a daze.
For who knew the depths had such fun,
With hats, socks, and dances undone!

Depths of Tranquility

A turtle once thought he could race,
But he took a nap, lost his place.
When finally stirred, he turned around,
Said, 'Next time, I'll sleep on the ground!'

The dolphins all laughed at his plight,
While spinning in circles, what a sight!
They splashed him awake with a cheer,
'Wake up, sleepyhead, the coast is clear!'

A crab with a monocle declared,
'In this calm, no one should be scared!'
But he tripped on a shell, fell outright,
And the fish all burst out with delight!

So in these depths, life zips, it flies,
With funny flops and joyful cries.
The ocean's quirks are quite the treat,
Where even naps can't be beat!

Nautical Nightfall

The octopus painted a mural wide,
With colors so bright, he needed some pride.
But one errant swipe smudged the art,
He exclaimed, 'That's just abstract, from the heart!'

A seahorse pranced, all dressed in flair,
He boasted his tail could dance in the air.
But a wave tossed him into the gloom,
Came up all tangled, looking like a broom!

Starry skies reflected on the tide,
While fish in bow ties felt dignified.
A crab yelled, 'Let's toast with some kelp!'
And all below giggled to the help!

So nightfall brings laughter, not dread,
With sea shenanigans spreading instead.
In depths where whimsy always takes flight,
The maritime fun sparks joy and delight!

Hidden Realms of the Reef

A clownfish wore shoes two sizes small,
He tripped over corals, began to sprawl.
'Fashion's pain!' he boldly proclaimed,
While the others all giggled, fully entertained.

The sea anemones had a little chat,
About whether crabs could wear a hat.
One crab snuck in and gave it a try,
But the hat was too big, oh my, oh my!

An eel, looking slick, threw a boogie down,
He shook, he twisted, King of the Crown!
But one sleek move slipped him on his tail,
And now all the fish tell the tale!

In realms where mischief swims with glee,
The laughter spreads wild and free.
For in each coral nook and fold,
Funny moments in the deep unfold!

Murmurs from the Abyssal Plains

In a world where fish wear shoes,
And crabs play cards with snails,
Jellyfish light the dance floor bright,
As seaweed sways and wails.

Starfish play chess on sandy beds,
While octopuses juggle shells,
Down here where laughter bubbles up,
And no one ever yells.

Turtles in bowties sip on tea,
While sharks are telling jokes,
The pufferfish's punchlines fly,
As bubbles burst with pokes.

Deep in the blue, the antics reign,
A whale that does a flip,
With silly grins and goofy spins,
It's quite a playful trip.

Dances of the Marine Spirits

In the coral palace, mermaids twirl,
With dolphins joining in a swirl,
They bust some moves with gliding grace,
While seahorses keep up the pace.

Clownfish wear frowns, they steal the scene,
As leafy seadragons dance in green,
With a wave of fins and giddy cheers,
They shimmy away all their fears.

A conch shell band plays tunes so fine,
A solo crab sings, "I'm doing just fine!"
The rhythm of waves, a calypso beat,
Underwater vibes that can't be beat.

So if you dive where the spirits sway,
You'll find some fun at the end of the bay,
With every flip and every spin,
You'll laugh until the day wears thin.

Underwater Reveries

In the deep where the fish wear wigs,
There's a party for the squids,
Dancing with a sense of flair,
As bubbles float through salty air.

The lobsters pull their best dance moves,
While shrimp do their groovy grooves,
A narwhal spins with a flick of horn,
Who knew the sea was never worn?

Anglerfish with glowing eyes,
Play hide and seek, what a surprise,
With giggles echoing near the reef,
They joke about the underwater beef.

So let the tides take you away,
To a realm where laughter likes to play,
In underwater dreams so absurd,
Where every moment's a funny word.

The Hidden Symphony of Waves

Beneath the foam, a symphony,
With sand dollars clinking happily,
The dolphins sing in perfect key,
While crabs whistle a melody.

Seashells chime in gentle tones,
As turtles tap on ocean bones,
Anemones sway to the bass,
With every wave, they find their place.

The fish all twirl in perfect time,
To a rhythm fresh as a lime,
While octopus conducts with flair,
As sea cucumbers are dancing there.

So listen close to the ocean's tune,
Near midday sun or under moon,
Where laughter drifts through salty air,
And playful spirits fill the fare.

www.ingramcontent.com/pod-product-compliance
Lightning Source LLC
Chambersburg PA
CBHW051736290426
43661CB00123B/561